W9-BOM-596

Fox River Valley PLD
555 Barrington Ave., Dundee, IL 60118
www.frvpld.info
Renew online or call 847-590-8706

My First Picture Encyclopedia

Show Me

POLAR ANIMALS

by Lisa J. Amstutz

Consultant:
Thomas Evans
Wildlife Biologist
U.S. Fish and Wildlife Service
Anchorage, Alaska

CAPSTONE PRESS
a capstone imprint

A+ Books are published by Capstone Press,
1710 Roe Crest Drive, North Mankato, Minnesota 56003.
www.capstonepub.com

Library of Congress Cataloging-in-Publication Data
Cataloging-in-publication information is on file with the Library of Congress.
ISBN 978-1-62065-059-2 (library binding)
ISBN 978-1-62065-920-5 (paper over board)
ISBN 978-1-4765-1332-4 (ebook PDF)

Editorial Credits
Mandy Robbins, editor; Heidi Thompson, designer; Svetlana Zhurkin, media researcher; Laura Manthe, production specialist

Photo Credits
Alamy: Papilio, 13 (middle), Wildlife GmbH, 27 (top); Digital Stock, 26 (top right); Dreamstime: Aquazoom, 26 (top left), Iakov Filimonov, 28 (left), Outdoorsman, 15 (bottom), Paul Loewen, 12 (bottom), Rambleon, 25 (middle left), Regatafly, 11 (middle left), Reinhardt, 13 (top), Thomas Barrat, 25 (bottom), Twildlife, 19 (middle right); iStockphotos: Karel Delvoye, 24 (top), Keith Szafranski, 29 (bottom); Library of Congress, 7 (top left and right); Minden Pictures: Matthias Breiter, 11 (top), 30 (bottom), Piotr Naskrecki, 21 (middle); National Geographic Stock: Bill Curtsinger, 21 (top left), 31 (top), Paul Nicklen, 13 (bottom), 17 (middle left); Newscom: Danita Delimont Photography/Jim Goldstein, 30 (top), Danita Delimont Photography/Paul Souders, 24 (bottom), Image Broker/Konrad Wothe, 17 (top), VWPics/David Fleetham, 14 (top), ZUMA Press/VWPics/Andy Murch, 16 (bottom left); Photo Researchers: Joseph T. Collins, 20 (top right); Shutterstock: Achim Baque, 9 (bottom left), ANCH, 17 (bottom left), Antonio Abrignani, 18 (bottom), AridOcean, 4–5, Arto Hakola, 18 (top left), Boris Pamikov, 17 (bottom right), Chris Pole, 27 (middle), Christopher Elwell, 15 (middle left), Cosmin Manci, 20 (bottom), Cynthia Kidwell, 26 (bottom), Dani Vincek, 16 (top), David Ashley, 31 (middle), Eric Isselée, 19 (middle left), 20 (top left), ericlefrancais, cover (bottom middle), FloridaStock, 12 (top), Gary Whitton, 6 (top), Gentoo Multimedia, 8, 29 (middle), George Burba, 6 (bottom), Gerald A. DeBoer, 21 (bottom), Henrik Larsson, 21 (top right), holbox, 17 (middle right), Iwona Grodzka (torn paper), cover, 1, Jamen Percy, 5 (right), 10 (top), Jan Martin Will, 22, JKlingebiel, 11 (bottom left), Juan Gracia, 15 (middle right), Keith Levit, 10 (bottom left), Lee Prince, 9 (top left), Leksele, 19 (top), Madlen, 25 (middle right), Mariusz Potocki, 31 (bottom), Maxim Kulko (wolf), back cover, 11, MCarter, 19 (bottom), Mike Liu, cover (bottom right), Miroslav Hlavko, back cover (top), 18 (top right), Monika Wieland, 14–15 (bottom), Natalia Bratslavsky, 15 (top), Nordroden, 9 (top right), papa1266, 16 (bottom right), Sergey Smolin, cover (top right), 1, Sergey Uryadnikov, 11 (bottom right), 28 (right), SH-Vector (snowflakes), cover, back cover, 1, 2–3, Sylvie Bouchard, cover (bottom left), 10 (bottom right), Vasiliy Koval, 11 (middle right), 23 (top), visceralimage, 23 (bottom), Vladimir Melnik, 4 (left), Volodymyr Goinyk, back cover (bottom middle and right), 9 (bottom right), 27 (bottom), Wild Arctic Pictures, 7 (bottom), 25 (top); Wikipedia: Uwe Kils, 16 (middle right)

Note to Parents, Teachers, and Librarians
My First Picture Encyclopedias provide an early introduction to reference materials for young children. These accessible, visual encyclopedias support literacy development by building subject-specific vocabularies and research skills. Stimulating format, inviting content, and phonetic aids assist and encourage young readers.

Printed in the United States of America in North Mankato, Minnesota.
092012   006933CGS13

Table of Contents

What Are Polar Animals?

Polar animals live near the North and South Poles. They live in the coldest places on Earth. Why are some animals more suited for living in these frozen lands? Let's find out.

Arctic
the area north of the Arctic Circle; much of the Arctic is an icy ocean

North Pole
the northern-most point on Earth

continent
one of the seven large land masses of Earth; Antarctica is a continent

South Pole
the southern-most point on Earth

Antarctica
the continent surrounding the South Pole; Antarctica is almost entirely covered with ice

Arctic Ocean

the ocean surrounding the North Pole; the Arctic Ocean is mostly covered with ice

Arctic Circle

an imaginary east-west line that circles the North Pole; areas north of the Arctic Circle have at least one day during the winter when the sun never rises

hemisphere

(HEM-uhss-fihr)—one half of the Earth; Antarctica is in the Earth's southern hemisphere, and the Arctic is in the northern hemisphere

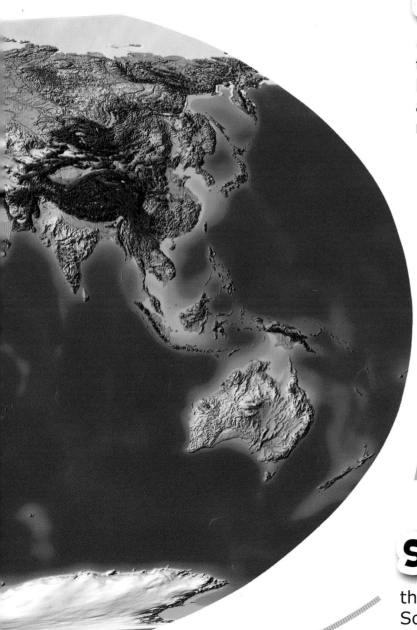

Antarctic Circle

an imaginary east-west line near Antarctica; areas south of the Antarctic Circle have at least one day during the winter when the sun never rises

Southern Ocean

the ocean surrounding Antarctica; the Southern Ocean is much larger and deeper than the Arctic Ocean

All about the Arctic and Antarctic

The wind howls across thick sheets of ice and snow. Temperatures drop far below freezing. Yet a few hardy plants and animals seem right at home in this extreme environment.

temperature

the measurement of how hot or cold something is; the coldest temperature ever measured on Earth was minus 128.6 degrees Fahrenheit (minus 89.2 degrees Celsius), in Antarctica

trees

only a few tiny trees grow in the Arctic; they spread out widely but are only a few inches high; no trees grow in the Antarctic

meltwater

water from melted snow and ice; in summer, meltwater forms marshes, lakes, and pools on the tundra; water does not drain away very quickly because the ground is always frozen a few inches below the surface

tundra

a cold area where large trees do not grow; the soil stays frozen just below the surface

explorer

a person who goes to an unknown place

- Norwegian explorer Roald Amundsen was the first person to reach the South Pole. He arrived with his team on December 14, 1911. They got there on skis with dogs pulling sleds full of supplies. A British team led by Captain Robert F. Scott arrived five weeks later.

- American Robert Peary is thought to be the first explorer to reach the North Pole. He and his team reached their destination in 1909. They traveled by dogsled.

ice sheet

a giant sheet of ice covering a large area of land; the Antarctic ice sheet is about the size of the United States and Mexico combined; the Greenland ice sheet, in the Arctic, is three times as big as Texas

northern lights

colored lights appearing in the sky near the North and South Poles; they are caused by gases in the air colliding with particles from the sun

polar desert

the Arctic and Antarctic are snowy deserts; very little snow or rain falls, and the freshwater stays frozen for much of the year

An Icy World

One of the most amazing things about the Arctic is the various types of ice there. Native Arctic people have many words to describe minor differences in ice conditions. They can determine whether it is safe to travel on ice. However, the conditions change frequently with winds and tidal currents.

 **fast ice**

sea ice that is "stuck fast" to the coast or ocean floor

 **glacier**

(GLAY-shur)—a large, slow-moving sheet of ice

pack ice

a large area of floating ice that is not attached to the shore

 lead

(LEED)—area of open water on a frozen body of water

permafrost

a layer of frozen earth underground that never thaws, even in summer; in many polar areas, permafrost is only a few inches below the surface

calving

the sudden breaking away of a large piece of a glacier

ice floe

a sheet of floating ice

iceberg

a huge piece of ice that floats in the ocean; icebergs break off from glaciers and ice sheets; only the tip of an iceberg is above water—the underwater part is much larger

polar ice pack

large areas of pack ice made from seawater; the Arctic ice pack covers the North Pole, and the Antarctic ice pack surrounds the Antarctic ice sheet

Land Mammals

Warm fur coats and layers of fat help land mammals survive cold Arctic temperatures. There are no land mammals in Antarctica. The Antarctic is too cold, and there is not enough food or shelter for mammals to survive on land.

wolverine

a large, fierce member of the weasel family; wolverines will attack large animals such as reindeer and elk

arctic fox

a small fox that lives in the Arctic; its fur is white in winter and brown in summer

caribou

(CARE-uh-boo)—a large member of the deer family; caribou have antlers and travel long distances across the Arctic tundra

arctic hare

a large, rabbitlike animal that lives in the Arctic; some arctic hares have white fur all year round while others turn brown in summer

gray wolf

the largest member of the dog family; wolves live and hunt in groups of two to 30, called packs

lemming

a small mammal with furry feet and a short tail; lemmings are an important food source for many animals including owls, weasels, and foxes

musk ox

a large, shaggy, cowlike animal; musk oxen dig through snow with their hooves to find roots and mosses

lynx

a grayish wildcat with long legs and tufts of fur on its ears; lynx live mainly in northern forests but are also found on the tundra

polar bear

a kind of bear that lives near the North Pole; polar bears travel over sea ice hunting seals

Playing It Safe

Danger lurks everywhere in icy lands. How do polar animals defend themselves? Check out some of their tricks.

claw

a hard curved nail on the foot of an animal; polar bears use both claws and teeth to hunt and defend themselves

teeth

the hard, white parts of the mouth used for biting and chewing food; walruses also use their very long teeth, called tusks, to defend themselves

speed

how fast something moves; arctic hares can run at speeds of up to 40 miles (64 kilometers) per hour when they are threatened

camouflage

a pattern or color on an animal's skin that makes it blend in with the things around it; the arctic hare's coat matches the snow in winter and the rocks in summer

antlers

bony structures that grow on some animals' heads; caribou use their antlers for fighting and defending their feeding areas

burrow

a hole in the ground made by an animal; ptarmigans (TAR-mi-guhns) often fly into snow banks to create small burrows; there they stay safe and warm

circle

musk oxen form a circle around their young when danger is near; they can toss a wolf in the air with their horns and then stomp on it

offspring

the young of a person, animal, or plant; some prey animals have many offspring to make sure some survive; lemmings give birth three or four times a year, with about five to six young in each litter, but many are eaten by owls, foxes, and birds called skuas

Marine Mammals

Not all polar mammals live on land. Some strong swimmers spend most or all of their lives in icy oceans. They come to the surface often to breathe. A thick layer of fat called blubber keeps them warm.

narwhal

a type of porpoise that lives in the Canadian Arctic; a male narwhal's sharp, twisted tusk grows up to 10 feet (3 meters) long

orca

a black and white whale that can weigh up to 10 tons (9 metric tons); orcas eat fish, seals, walruses, and even other whales; they can be found in both the Arctic and Antarctic; orcas are the largest members of the dolphin family

seal

a sea mammal that has thick fur and flippers and lives in coastal waters; native peoples have traditionally hunted seals for food, clothing, fuel, and more; many species of seals live in the polar ice-covered areas

sea lion

a large seal with earflaps; sea lions can walk on all four flippers

walrus

a large seal with two long ivory teeth called tusks; its tusks help it climb out of the water, break holes in the ice, and fight with other walruses

whale

a large mammal that lives in the ocean and breathes through a blowhole; a thick layer of blubber keeps the whale warm and helps it float; porpoises and dolphins are subgroups of the whale family

Out to Sea

Despite harsh conditions, polar oceans are full of life. Many kinds of sea animals, from tiny krill to giant squid, live in the Arctic and Antarctic.

clam

a small ocean animal that lives inside a shell; clamshells are hard to open

icefish

an Antarctic fish with white blood; icefish can survive in temperatures that would normally cause blood to freeze

Greenland shark

the most northern of all the sharks; its meat is poisonous if eaten fresh but can be eaten safely when cooked or dried

crab

an animal with 10 legs; two legs are hidden under its shell; the Alaskan king crab can grow as large as a tractor tire

krill

a sea animal with many feathery legs that help it swim; the average krill is about the size of your pinky finger; a blue whale can eat 4 tons (3.6 metric tons) of krill per day

arctic cod

a fish that lives in the Arctic Ocean; antifreeze chemicals in its blood keep it from freezing in the cold water

squid

a sea animal with a long, soft body and eight or 10 fingerlike limbs used to grasp food; squid can spurt out "ink" when fleeing a predator; many can also change colors

starfish

a star-shaped animal found in many oceans, including the Arctic; starfish usually have five arms and bumpy or spiny skin

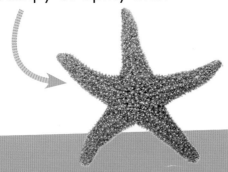

jellyfish

a sea animal with tentacles and a soft, almost clear body

Feathered Friends

Birds live in polar areas too. Some stay all year. Others migrate to warmer places in winter. All birds have feathers. But not all of them can fly.

arctic tern

a bird that nests and spends the summer in the Arctic, then flies south for another summer in the Antarctic; the arctic tern migrates farther than any other bird—44,000 miles (71,000 km) per year

skua

a large seabird similar to a gull; skuas are sometimes called the "pirates of the skies" because they steal fish from other birds; they also snatch young birds of other species from their nests

great auk

a large, flightless bird that was hunted for its meat, oil, and feathers until it died out and became extinct; smaller auks still live in the Arctic and can fly

penguin

a black and white bird with short legs; penguins cannot fly, but their wings help them glide through the water; penguins live only in the southern hemisphere

ptarmigan

a ground-dwelling bird in the tundra; ptarmigans scratch for seeds and buds under the snow; they grow white feathers and extra feathers on their feet in winter

snowy owl

a large owl that lives in the Arctic tundra; it grows white feathers in winter; snowy owls hunt lemmings and can hear one moving under 1 foot (30.5 centimeters) of snow

tundra swan

a large water bird that migrates south for the winter; tundra swans were once called whistling swans because the flapping of their wings makes a whistling sound

19

Small Fry

Polar animals tend to be larger than similar animals in warmer climates because larger bodies lose less heat. But small animals find ways to keep warm in the Arctic and Antarctic too.

adder

a venomous snake; most reptiles cannot survive in polar areas, but adders are sometimes found north of the Arctic Circle

ice worm

the only worm that lives in ice; ice worms are just 0.4 inch (1 cm) long and feed on tiny plants in the snow called algae

butterfly

a thin insect with large, colored wings; butterflies live nearly everywhere in the world except Antarctica; arctic butterflies grow very slowly; most take more than a year to develop

Siberian salamander

a four-legged animal with soft, moist skin and a long tail; it spends part of its life in water and can survive being frozen for long periods of time

midge

a tiny insect in the fly family; though less than 0.25 inch (0.6 cm) long, a wingless midge is the largest land animal found in Antarctica

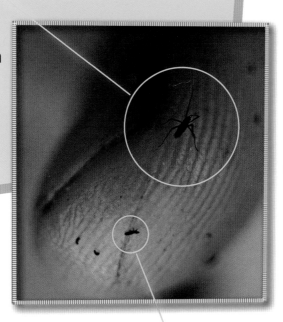

mosquito

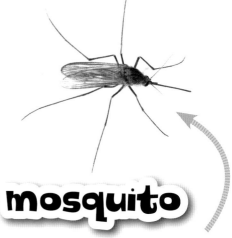

a small, flylike insect; females feed on the blood of birds and mammals and sometimes carry diseases

tundra bumblebee

a large, hairy bee; tundra bumblebees have extra hair to keep them warm; shivering their muscles warms them up enough to fly

springtail

a small, wingless insect with a forklike organ on its underside that helps it leap into the air; in polar areas, springtails are known as snow fleas

wood frog

the only frog that can survive in the far north; wood frogs freeze solid during the winter, and their heart and lungs stop; in spring, they thaw out again and keep hopping

Staying Warm

Polar animals don't need mittens or boots to stay warm. Their bodies are well adapted to their cold, icy homes. Each body part has a special purpose.

feathers

light, flat structures that cover a bird's body; the penguin has thick, oily feathers that keep water and cold air out; penguins have more feathers than most birds

down

the soft, fluffy feathers of a bird; downy tufts at the base of each penguin feather add warmth

color

dark colors absorb more heat from the sun; light colors match the snow and sky; a swimming penguin is hard to see from above because its dark back blends in with the water; it is hard to see from below because its white belly blends in with the white sky and ice

blubber

a thick layer of fat under the skin of some animals such as penguins, whales, and polar bears; blubber keeps animals warm

antifreeze

a chemical that keeps water from freezing; people put antifreeze in their cars to keep their engines from freezing in winter; many polar fish have antifreeze chemicals in their blood

hoof

the hard covering on an animal's foot; the sharp edges on musk ox hooves keep them from slipping on the ice

guard hair

long, coarse outer hairs; a musk ox's guard hairs grow up to 28 inches (71 cm) long; they help keep out snow and hold in heat

ear

a body part used for hearing; arctic foxes have fur on the outside and inside of their short ears to keep their ears from freezing

underfur

a short, thick layer of fur under the guard hairs that adds extra warmth

tail

the part at the back end of an animal's body; the arctic fox has a thick, furry tail, also called a brush; when it gets very cold, the fox curls up and wraps its tail around itself

nose

a body part used for smelling and breathing; arctic foxes have short noses; their small size helps hold in heat

hibernate

to spend winter in a deep sleep; winter in the Arctic and Antarctic is too long and cold for most animals to hibernate, but arctic ground squirrels and a few other animals sleep for long periods of time

Dinner Time

Each animal has its own unique diet. Some polar animals eat meat. Others prefer plants. And some eat a little bit of both.

food chain

series of organisms in which each living thing eats the one before it

prey

an animal hunted by another animal for food; cod are prey for seals, and seals are prey for polar bears

predator

an animal that hunts other animals for food; the seal, polar bear, and arctic fox are predators

scavenger

an animal that feeds on animals that are already dead; the arctic fox often follows a polar bear and eats food the bear leaves behind

omnivore

an animal that eats both plants and animals; the arctic fox is an omnivore because it feeds on animals as well as berries and seaweed

graze

to eat grass and other plants; reindeer graze on reindeer moss and other small plants

herbivore

an animal that eats only plants; reindeer are herbivores

carnivore

an animal that eats meat; wolves are carnivores

reindeer moss

a lichen with branches that look like reindeer antlers; a lichen is a fungus with a tiny plant growing inside it

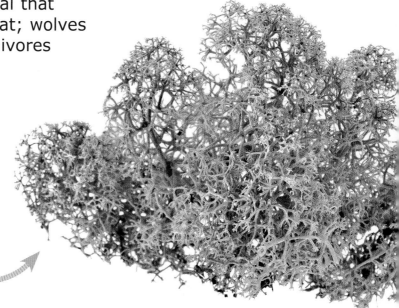

breathing holes

holes in the ice made by seals so they can come up for air; polar bears wait by breathing holes when they hunt seals

Let's Talk

Whistle, bark, howl, hiss! Animals have many ways of communicating. Some make noises. Others use signals or even smells.

chatter

to make fast, speechlike sounds; weasels sometimes chatter to each other

echolocation

(eh-koh-loh-KAY-shuhn) the process of using sounds and echoes to find objects; whales and dolphins use echolocation to find food

hiss

to make an "sss" sound like a snake; polar bears may hiss when they are angry

howl

to make a loud, long "oow" noise; wolves howl to communicate with each other

whistle

to make a clear, musical sound through the lips or teeth; sea otters may whistle when frustrated or upset

roar

to make a loud, deep growling noise; male hooded seals roar during mating season

scent

the smell of an animal, often used to mark its territory or attract a mate; musk oxen get their name from the musky-smelling urine they spray on their long hair

bellow

to shout or roar; musk oxen can bellow like cows

ear or tail position

some animals, such as wolves, can communicate by moving their ears or tails; many animals will put their ears back when alarmed, scared, or threatened

bird songs

birds sing to communicate to possible mates and for defense and alarm calls

bark

the short, loud sound a dog makes; arctic foxes can bark like dogs

Polar Babies

Growing up in the Arctic or Antarctic can be tough. Polar parents work hard to keep their babies warm and safe.

den

a place where a wild animal may live; a female polar bear digs a den in the snow before giving birth; the den keeps cubs warm and safe

life cycle

the series of changes a living thing goes through from birth to death

breed

to mate or produce young

cub

a young polar bear; newborn cubs weigh about 1.5 pounds (680 grams)

litter

a group of animals born at one time to one mother; polar bears usually have two cubs in a litter

nest

a place where insects, birds, or animals lay eggs or give birth to young; some penguins make nests of pebbles while others make no nests at all

egg

a rounded object with a covering or shell in which young animals develop; female birds lay eggs

hatch

to break out of an egg

brood pouch

a flap of skin on a parent's belly that it uses to wrap around an egg; a penguin's egg or chick rests snugly in a brood pouch on its parent's feet

rookery

a breeding place or colony of birds or animals; penguins lay their eggs in a rookery

crèche

(KRESH)—a large group of young animals who are cared for by some, but not all, of the parents; penguin chicks often live together in a crèche

chick

a young bird

Travel Time

Some polar animals are world travelers. Others stay close to home. Polar animals move about in many ways.

walk

caribou walk up to 3,100 miles (5,000 km) between their breeding grounds and winter feeding grounds every year; sharp edges on their hooves prevent them from slipping on ice and rocks

migrate

to move from one place to another; many polar animals migrate to warmer climates to find food and to avoid harsh winter conditions

hop

arctic hares hop on their hind legs when being chased; they can move at more than 37 miles (60 km) per hour

snowshoes

light, netted frames that attach to a person's feet and let them walk on top of the snow; a caribou's wide hooves act like snowshoes

swim

to move through water; moose are excellent swimmers because their wide hooves act as paddles

breach

to jump out of the water; even some of the largest whales can hurl themselves out of the water

dive

to plunge underwater; seals can dive longer and deeper than most mammals

rocketing

to shoot straight into the air when jumping out of the water; some penguins can rocket 6 feet (1.8 m) in the air

spyhop

when a whale turns upright with its head out of the water; the whale treads water with its flippers as it checks out the surface

tobogganing

when a penguin slides on its belly across the ice

Read More

Green, Jen. *Life on the Tundra.* Nature in Focus:
New York: Gareth Stevens Pub., 2010.

Parker, Steve. *Polar Regions. Planet Earth*
Laguna Hills, Calif.: QEB Publishing, 2008.

Wilsdon, Christina. *Polar Bears.* Amazing Animals.
Pleasantville, N.Y.: Gareth Stevens Pub., 2009

Titles in this set:

Show Me
COMMUNITY HELPERS

Show Me
DINOSAURS

Show Me
DOGS

Show Me
INSECTS

Show Me
POLAR ANIMALS

Show Me
REPTILES

Show Me
SPACE

Show Me
TRANSPORTATION

Internet Sites

FactHound offers a safe, fun way to find Internet sites related to this book. All of the sites on FactHound have been researched by our staff.

Here's all you do:

Visit *www.facthound.com*

Type in this code: 9781620650592

Super-cool stuff! Check out projects, games and lots more at
www.capstonekids.com